WHEN YOU CATCH THE VISION

O. Emmanuel Sokefun

Unless otherwise indicated, all Bible verses in this book are quoted from the King James version of the Bible.

ISBN (eBook):
ISBN (Paperback): 979-8845667861
ISBN (Hardcover): 979-8845691125

You can contact the author via eaibukunoluwa@gmail.com.

*Dedicated to everyone who has endured difficulties
in bringing their God-given vision to reality.*

CONTENTS

BLANK PAGE

INTRODUCTION

Text:

And when he [Herod] *had apprehended him* [Peter], *he put him in prison, and delivered him to four quaternions of soldiers to keep him; intending after Easter to bring him forth to the people.*

Peter therefore was kept in prison: but prayer was made without ceasing of the church unto God for him.

And as Peter knocked at the door of the gate, a damsel came to hearken, named Rhoda.

And when she knew Peter's voice, she opened not the gate for gladness, but ran in, and told how Peter stood before the gate.

And they said unto her, Thou art mad. But she constantly affirmed that it was even so. Then said they, It is his angel.

But Peter continued knocking: and when they had opened the door, and saw him, they were astonished.

(Acts 12:4,5,13-16)

A vision is a special solution that you want to be delivered. In the Bible text, Peter had been arrested by Herod and was scheduled for execution. Therefore, desperate members of the Church gathered in the house of Mary the mother of John to pray for his release. That was their earnest cry and heart's desire. Peter, therefore, symbolises the "vision" which they wanted to be manifested. The church caught a vision that their General Overseer will return to them unharmed. They sought that vision, prayed for it, and waited for it. While they were gathered in prayer, God sent an angel to Peter's prison and set him loose in the middle of the night. Thus, in the dead of the night, Peter made his way to the house where they were praying for him, to join up with them.

After knocking at the door, a lady called Rhoda came and opened the door for Peter. We will call her the person who pioneered the vision because she was the first person who took steps to let in the vision. The entire scenario, including her reaction and subsequent events that followed, contains 15 important lessons for us to learn concerning the manifestation of our vision. These will be discussed in different chapters of this book.

LESSON 1: A VISION IS BIRTHED IN YOUR AREA OF DESPERATION

Peter therefore was kept in prison: but prayer was made without ceasing of the church unto God for him.

(Acts 12:5)

Like the story of the Church that gathered to pray for the release of Peter, God gives you a vision often through areas that you are most desperate to see a change. That was all they wanted. Sometimes, you feel as if some part of you has been locked and needs to be unleashed. You feel as if you are not operating at maximum capacity. You feel that something is lacking in your environment, state, or country. You wish that something should be done to address the situation urgently. People (including you) may not recognise, acknowledge, or understand it, but this area of desperation, frustration, and pain, is often your God-given vision.

"The vision" goes beyond getting rich, owning property, and driving exotic cars. It is deeper than having people at your beck and call. It is a calling, a solution, an idea that transcends your whims and cravings. It is a call to serve. It places impact above income. God puts this desire there for us to solve problems in our world and make it a better place.

Moses saw the great torment that the Israelites suffered in Egypt. He was desperate to see them free from Egyptian bondage and tyranny (Exodus 2). The Bible says that **"it came into his heart"** to help their affliction. Consider that statement. To "come in" indicates an entry from the outside. It was not his own thought and it did not generate in his mind. The door of his mind opened and it entered into his mind from the outside like a visitor. As we would later realise, it was God that opened his mind and planted in the vision.

And when he was full forty years old, <u>it came into his heart</u> to visit his brethren the children of Israel.

(Acts 7:23)

To others, he was just an overzealous patriot—or worse. He was even challenged by the very Israelites that he fought for. No one understood that the vision was from God. That is what this book is helping you to understand about you and others. What enters into your heart and burdens you about your society and our world?

And seeing one of them suffer wrong, he defended him, and avenged him that was oppressed, and smote the Egyptian:

<u>For he supposed his brethren would have understood how that God by his hand would deliver them: but they understood not</u>.

(Acts 7:24-25)

God had put the desire in Moses, to liberate Israel and relocate them to the Promised Land.

Going into Labour Before You Get Pregnant

Psalms 7:14 looks strange at first glance, and it is an example of how your vision comes.

Behold, [1] he travaileth... and [2] hath conceived... and [3] brought forth...

(Psalms 7:14)

In the natural, for a woman to give birth, she must get pregnant (conceive) first. Then she must carry the pregnancy to term. After bringing the pregnancy to term, she goes into labour (travail), and then she delivers (brings forth) (Figure 1).

Figure 1: Sequence of events in child delivery in the natural world.

But in Psalms 7:14, we see that a person who brought his vision to pass first TRAVAILED before even conceiving a seed! That is, he experienced pain, disappointment, disillusionment, and frustration. He saw needs in society that had to be met. He saw injustice, lack, deficiencies, and opportunities that needed to be plugged in very quickly (Figure 2).

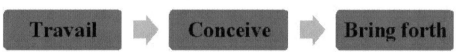

Figure 2: Common sequence of events in delivering a vision.

While travailing, he CONCEIVED an idea (the vision). He imagined, "Imagine if someone stepped up and corrected this problem, how much improvement it will bring to our society. I long to see this done."

The word used for "imagination" in the Bible, is the Hebrew word "yetser", which means "conceive". So, when you imagine something, you are conceiving an idea or potential solution. Many of the visionaries and inventors of the world caught a vision that way. Someone said, "I cannot stand this daily darkness whenever night falls. We can have an alternative source of light apart from the sun. In the process of exploration, electricity-powered light was invented. Today, the whole world is enjoying the benefits of that vision that came from conceiving after travailing.

LESSON 2: THE VISION IS IMPRISONED!

And when he [Herod] had apprehended him [Peter],
he put him in prison, and delivered him to four
quaternions of soldiers to keep him…

(Acts 12:4)

Implementing your vision will give you an amazing sense of fulfilment while you impact your world. But there is a war against your vision! So many factors are out there to make sure that you never see your vision. Some people slump into a life of routine or pleasure and forfeit the vision they were meant to discover. The majority of the people in our world are like that and that is why the bottom is always crowded.

Dr Myles Munroe put it this way, "The graveyard is the richest place on earth because there you will see the books that were never published, ideas that were not harnessed, songs that were not sung, and drama pieces that were never acted."

Why? Because most people refuse to act upon the imaginations they conceive in their hearts until they die. The vision needs to be discovered. And after discovering it, you must put in the effort. Because people are unwilling to put in this effort, they let their vision and potentials go to waste. Your vision never falls on your lap like a ripe cherry. This will distinguish serious people who put in the work from chickens that scratch the ground for food.

We read that Peter the "vision" was locked up in a prison and kept in the care of four quaternions of soldiers. A quaternion is a group of four soldiers. Peter, a single, unarmed, nonviolent man, was delivered into the hands of FOUR quaternions (sixteen) of Roman soldiers just for the words he spoke! Anyone who wanted to set him free would have had quite a task on their hands!

When Peter slept, he was bound with two strong chains and kept in the middle of two soldiers! They did not even leave him alone in the prison to himself after binding his hands and feet in shackles! They did not want to take chances of Peter escaping from the prison in one way or another. They were determined to deliver him to Herod for execution. Additionally, there were guards surrounding the prison.

And when Herod would have brought him forth, the same night Peter was sleeping between two soldiers, bound with two chains: and the keepers before the door kept the prison.

(Acts 12:6)

The prison cell is like the mind of a man, where ideas are trapped. The chains represent obstacles and forces that repress the expression of your potentials and prevent you from obtaining the vision. They may be negative personality traits. Laziness, fear, idleness, doubt, procrastination, addiction, peer pressure, pride, wastefulness, a carefree life, rudeness, lone-ranging, gluttony, greed, and deceit, are examples of chains that bind a man's progress on the way to his vision. We would have to defeat them one after the other and continuously to free our vision from prison. The chains on his hands are wasters of efforts while the chains on the feet are hinderances to progress. The soldiers inside the cell represent enemies within your camp whose task is to ensure you never make headway. The external soldiers may be external influences like haters, your background, detractors, workers of darkness, or demons. They may be sicknesses or diseases or any such thing that want the vision to die in your mind.

The vision never manifests without you overcoming these factors. Observe the lives of those who seemed to chance upon a discovery. You will see years of overcoming their chains and soldiers before that moment. You will discover that majority of them were even in the place of labour when they came upon the idea that blew up their lives.

It is said that Professor Alexander Fleming discovered antibiotics by chance. One day in his laboratory, as he was about to throw away a Petri dish that he used to grow bacteria, he noticed something unusual on it. A mould from nearby had blown into his lab and contaminated his bacterial growth. He noticed that bacteria did not grow around the spot where the mould grew. That puzzled him. He realised then that he had just discovered an organism that inhibits the growth of bacteria (an antibiotic). He tried growing this mould with bacteria over and over, and the results were the same—bacteria never grew around the mould. He named this antibiotic penicillin, and over time, he discovered several other antibiotics.

Professor Fleming was not a lucky man. First, he had overcome his ignorance. If any random person saw the same mould growing around bacteria, it would have meant nothing to them and they would have discarded the Petri dish. Moreover, Professor Fleming was not a lazy man. He had spent many years in the lab experimenting on microbiology. He was not in his house when he discovered penicillin. He discovered penicillin on a culture plate in his lab. Before discovering penicillin, he had discovered the enzyme lysozyme by a similar chance event in the lab. On both occasions, he was at work. Professor Fleming was a diligent man, and that gave him an advantage in the race towards his world-changing discoveries. And after discovering this antibiotic, he spent several years of research carefully studying what he found.

How could a man like Nikola Tesla have registered over a thousand patents in his name if he spent his entire time partying and watching reality shows? Yet, someone will sit on a couch watching the TV for hours and lament how they never make headway in life.

Bishop David Oyedepo said, "Those who often appear on TV hardly have time to watch it." The summary of this lesson is that even after you conceive, you must overcome your demons and be ready to put in the work to actualise your vision.

LESSON 3: DISBAND YOUR QUATERNIONS

Peter therefore was kept in prison: but prayer was made without ceasing of the church unto God for him.

(Acts 12:5)

In the case of Peter in the Bible text, the Church realised that for them to get the vision they desired, they had to pray fervently. They prayed night and day for God to intervene and that proved pivotal in this story. Do you want to see your vision manifest? Be a man or woman of diligent prayer. Your mouth is powerful. When you pray, you are speaking things forth and they begin to obey and align. Prayer is a way to remove spiritual obstacles hindering your vision. The combination of fervent prayer and fervent work will open doors to you that you never could have imagined walking through.

Commit thy works unto the LORD, and thy thoughts shall be established.

(Proverbs 16:3)

Moreover, prayer in this context represents the efforts you make to overcome your quaternions of soldiers. It symbolises the discipline and time spent in breaking the hold of a limiting mindset. It represents the hours of labour, study, sacrifice, and investment you put into bringing your dream to reality.

Your effort towards breaking the resistance holding your vision is not a one-time affair. You must commit yourself to it every day. Whenever doubt comes to your mind, resist it with words of affirmation. Whenever you find yourself engaging in habits that will sabotage your vision, you must immediately retrace your steps. If you have a problem that you cannot overcome alone, seek professional and spiritual help to overcome it before it overcomes you and kills you with your vision. As long as you are alive, you must always confront your soldiers physically, mentally, and spiritually. Keep praying and your vision will be easier to actualise.

Even Jesus had to overcome His soldiers before He could obtain the glory. Jesus had a God complex. He saw Himself as being equal to God. It is difficult to yield to man's authority and ill treatment when you are aware that you and God are equal. You will be severely tempted to employ your power to put your antagonists in their place.

Who [Jesus], *being in the form of God, thought it not robbery to be equal with God:*

(Philippians 2:5-6)

Jesus had to overcome this God complex because of the vision He carried. He had to take upon Him the mindset of a man and a servant of men. That was the only way He could have endured all the evil that was done to Him. He humbled Himself. This means that the humility was not automatic. He had to put Himself through the process rigorously and continuously. He also MADE HIMSELF of no reputation.

But made himself of no reputation, and took upon him the form of a servant, and was made in the likeness of men: And being found in fashion as a man, he humbled himself, and became obedient unto death, even the death of the cross.

(Philippians 2:7-8)

He carried the vision of being highly exalted by God and sitting on the right hand of the Father. If He had not defeated His God complex and yielded to the death on the cross, He would have had no opportunity to resurrect in glory, and no exaltation. His name would never have been exalted above every other name. After defeating His soldiers and completed the humiliating process, He obtained the vision.

Wherefore God also hath highly exalted him, and given him a name which is above every name: That at the name of Jesus every knee should bow, of things in heaven, and things in earth, and things under the earth; And that every tongue should confess that Jesus Christ is Lord, to the glory of God the Father.

(Philippians 2:9-11)

LESSON 4: NOTHING HAPPENS UNTIL SOMETHING MOVES

And, behold, the angel of the Lord came upon him, and a light shined in the prison: and he smote Peter on the side, and raised him up, saying, Arise up quickly. And his chains fell off from his hands.

(Acts 12:7)

When God answered the prayers of the Church, He sent an angel to Peter's cell. This represents God's divine guidance and help in response to our prayer. When the angel entered the prison, there was a great light of divine presence. Light, which dispels darkness, represents God's subduing of evil forces for us. Light also represents divine revelation and inspiration in our minds. This light, or inspiration, is the starting point of any new project. When God wanted to start creating the earth, He first called forth light (Genesis 1:3). You also derive strength and courage to pursue God's agenda when you pray. That is the beauty of prayer.

But notice the angel did not pamper Peter. He did not say, "Sorry, Peter, what a rough day you've had! Let me fly you home on Angel 747 Airways." Instead, the holy angel SMACKED Peter out of his sleep. The word used in waking him is "**smote**", which implies the application of force. It is synonymous to "smack", "strike", "beat" and "slap".

*...and he **smote** Peter on the side, and raised him up...*

(Acts 12:7)

Whenever "smite", "smote", or "smitten" is written in the Bible, it is used when you deal a grievous blow to hurt or kill a person. Consider three other Bible verses with the same word "smote", as examples.

*And God was **displeased** with this thing; therefore he **smote** Israel.*

(I Chronicles 21:7)

*Who **smote** the firstborn of Egypt, both of man and beast.*

(Psalms 135:8)

*And immediately the angel of the Lord **smote** him [Herod] because he gave not God the glory: and he was eaten of worms, and gave up the ghost.*

(Acts 12:23)

Smiting is a very unfriendly act! The angel actually rough handled Peter. He gave no illusion that he was there to pamper and cuddle him. He was there for serious business. God is displeased when our vision remains idle. He wants to kick it into gear. God will help you light your cell (give inspiration and revelation in your mind, and protection from the wicked), strengthen you to get up, and guide through instructions. And He will hide you from the guards (cover you from the enemies within and without). But pampering you is out of the picture. The angel did not even wait for Peter to wake up. As he struck him at his side, he grabbed him and pulled him to his feet. Apparently, Peter was too slow for the angel's liking!

While the angel was pulling him up, he ordered, "Get up quickly!!" That is God giving you the first push and an encouraging hand to help you stand. God initiates the process. He will wake you up and, with His hand, He will put you at the starting point where you can stand strong. But from then on, He expects you to grow up, man up, and get to work. He will not do your work for you.

When Peter was on his feet, he had not even uttered a word when the angel ordered again, "Gird yourself and wear your sandals." When Peter obeyed, another instruction followed, "Wear your coat and follow me" (Acts 12:8). It is not God's style to give all the details or instructions at once. He tells you in bits. He wants to see your obedience to the last instruction before committing the next set of instructions to you. But that is beside the point.

My main emphasis here is that the angel told Peter to do these things **by himself**, without any form of assistance. No one is going to pamper you, friend. It is your responsibility to get your vision moving after God initiates it. Thinking, planning and working on your own vision are your responsibility, not another's.

And the angel said unto him, <u>Gird thyself</u>, and <u>bind on thy sandals</u>. And so he did. And he saith unto him, <u>Cast thy garment about thee</u>, and follow me.

(Acts 12:8)

Many Christians miss it here. They expect God to arrive with His glory light, kiss them, tie their shoelaces, and carry them delicately on the wings of an angel to their comfortable bed at home while they remain asleep. If Christianity were that sweet, James would not have been killed, and Peter would not have been in prison in the first place. No one is spared the hard work, Christian or not.

The Limitations in Your Path

Remember, Peter's hands and feet were chained. How would he move? The chains did not fall off when the angel came in and a glorious light shone in the prison. The chains did not fall off when the angel smacked Peter. Peter would have expected the angel to unlock or break his chains, but he did not. Rather, we see another important principle here: **as Peter got on his feet**, his chains broke loose. What does that tell you? When he made effort to move forward, God backed up his effort and the limitations were surmounted. If you sit all day waiting for a miracle, you will get none. Your miracle will come when you are on the move. You must take the step of faith.

...<u>and raised him up</u>, saying, Arise up quickly. <u>And his chains fell off from his hands</u>.

(Acts 12:7)

As if to establish this principle, there was another gate on the way out of the prison. Expectedly, it was locked. But when Peter and the angel got there, it opened on its own. If Peter had remained in the cell, waiting for something to be done BEFORE he moved, he would have waited longer. Take steps of faith in the direction of your vision and mountains will move.

When they were past the first and the second ward, <u>they came unto the iron gate that leadeth unto the city; which opened to them of his own accord</u>: and they went out, and passed on through one street; and forthwith the angel departed from him.

(Acts 12:10)

"I have no money to pursue this idea. I'm waiting for one blessed day when good money will come." You're wasting your time. The money is out there. You may not get it at once, and you may not get it immediately, but it comes with making moves. You have a bigger chance getting a big job if you go out there and take a smaller job with lesser pay than if you wait for the big one to come suddenly. Where will your work experience come from to land the big job? If you need a huge sum, get to work and start saving and investing little by little. One day, you will get there. You may even strike a huge deal one day while working on the small ones. But you will strike no deal if you sit in your house waiting for something. Money goes where value is given in the form of goods and services. It avoids those who sit down waiting for a miracle.

We all celebrate David the great king. But David was not born a king and he did not start life as a king. He started with a small and lonely job as a shepherd boy. I'm sure he did not get paid because it was his father's flock. His feeding, clothing and shelter came from his father, and that would have been sufficient payment for his son. Then David took a job as a harpist to the mentally unstable king. At some point while David was being hunted by Saul, he took a security officer gig with his men under a wicked boss called Nabal. David never sat down waiting for the promise of becoming king of Israel. No, he went and did whatever he could find at the moment until the promise came. And you know what? Those small jobs prepared him for the big one!

"I've hit a roadblock, I can't move forward!" You can wait forever at the roadblock or you can take a step of faith and see how miraculously the problem will be solved! Like Peter, your chains will only fall off when you take that step.

What many people call faith is not faith at all. They sit down in their comfort zone after praying, expecting miracle money or opportunities to knock on their door. Faith is not sitting down and refusing to take a step or waiting for a rich uncle to give you money. Faith is getting up to take a little step despite all your limitations, because you believe that your little step will be met halfway by God's great step. Diligence and willingness to move forward in spite of circumstances characterise faith, not idle waiting. The chains of a lazy man will remain for long. A miracle comes to those who go forward in faith.

Have you been wondering why your prayers are not getting answered even though you are waiting for that limitation to go away? It is because you are doing exactly that—**waiting** for the limitation to go away. When the Israelites were waiting and crying at the Red Sea, God said to Moses, "Why are you crying to me? Tell them to forward." To ask Moses, "Why are you crying?" is to say that he was doing the wrong and unnecessary thing. It's as if Moses was being scolded for standing in one place and crying. It sounds like, "Why are you crying and disturbing me?! Tell them to move forward!". He expected Moses to know that they ought to move forward and not stand there wailing forever. Eventually, the power of God was activated when God's people moved forward in faith, not when they stood there crying.

And the LORD said unto Moses, <u>Wherefore criest thou unto me? speak unto the children of Israel, that they go forward</u>: But lift thou up thy rod, and stretch out thine hand over the sea, and divide it: and the children of Israel shall go on dry ground through the midst of the sea.

(Exodus 14:15-16)

Enemies cannot stop you because God is with you. We hear no mention of the soldiers in Peter's jail stopping Peter. It is when you are afraid and you crouch between them that they have power over you. When you rise up and leave the cell, they lose their power over you. The vision went easily past the internal and external enemies when it was put in motion after intense prayer. But until the vision is set in motion, chains and gates will not give way. Albert Einstein's statement best summarises this lesson: "Nothing happens until something moves."

LESSON 5: THE VISION OFTEN KNOCKS IN AN UNEXPECTED MANNER

And as Peter knocked at the door of the gate...

(Acts 12:13)

The main prayer of the Church would have been, "Oh God, touch Herod's heart and make him release Peter!" Never in their wildest imagination would they have anticipated that Peter would be released with power by an angel at night. As we read on in later verses, it was hard for the Church to believe. Peter himself Peter thought he was in a vision! Would you imagine the shock of the praying Church when the visitor knocking at 12:30 a.m. turned out to be Peter?! I would have been shocked if I was there!

We must understand from this account that visionary and revolutionary ideas often come to us at a time and place that we least expect them. You may go on a personal retreat and meditate all day long, but no idea comes. But when you are casually talking with someone or doing something mundane, an unusual idea you never considered drops in your heart.

It is said that Sir Isaac Newton was sitting in his garden and just meditating one day when an apple randomly fell from a tree in his garden. He pondered on this phenomenon and the aftermath of it was the propounding of Newton's Law of Universal Gravitation. There is nothing spectacular about apples falling off a tree. Apples fell every day in his garden, and he must have overlooked them. But something about that mundane event unlocked the discovery of a universal law. I am sure he never thought that one day he would have discovered anything special about the apples that fell every day and littered his premises. But that is how visionary ideas often come. You need to be flexible and open for you to identify opportunities that come knocking.

The fathers of old in the Bible caught the vision they had been seeking by having an open mind to the seemingly unspectacular. They were able to recognise something deep from the mundane, and in the end, they actualised the vision. Father Abraham knew this secret long ago. At the age of seventy-five, He caught the divine vision that he will have his special son through whom God will bring His covenant to pass. Years passed. Precisely, twenty-four years passed! A lot of water passed under the bridge during this time. The separation of Abraham and Lot. The war to save Lot from Chedorlaomer king of Elam and his allies. The birth of Ishmael. The dismissal of Hagar. A change of name for Abraham and Sarah. The covenant of circumcision. These were highlights of the gap period. Abraham prayed and waited on God for many years, yet the promise (vision) never manifested.

On a hot Arabian afternoon, three men stopped around Abraham's house looking unspectacular (Genesis 18). They were travellers with dusty feet. But Abraham knew this principle which you are now learning—that your vision can appear in a most unexpected way—and he sprang out of his house to usher them in. A wealthy man of ninety-nine years old bowed before three hungry-looking strangers with dusty feet. In the end, it was his miracle. It turned out that God and two angels visited Abraham and he received them well. He and his wife were blessed, and Isaac was born the following year.

Be not forgetful to entertain strangers: for thereby some have entertained angels unawares.

(Hebrews 13:2)

Whether literal or figurative angels, we should be flexible and receptive because you never know if your vision or helpers of your vision will locate you through the simple and mundane. Do not close your heart to spontaneous inspirations. You may be in the kitchen, on the move, in the bathroom, or in the middle of a movie or book when a sudden inspiration hits you for a solution that your world needs, or for a business idea. Welcome it, accept it, embrace it, nurture it, pray about it, and run with it.

Of course, there are times when the vision comes at the time, place, and moment that you expect. But history tells us that this is not often the case. Random conversations with people, casual strolling down the street, unplanned meetings, and sudden recollections of events may be ways in which supernatural ideas come to your mind.

LESSON 6: THE VISION COMES TO MANY PEOPLE AT THE SAME TIME BUT IS IGNORED BY MOST

And as Peter knocked at the door of the gate, a [one]
damsel came to hearken, named Rhoda.

(Acts 12:13)

Peter the "vision" knocked on the door of the gate while everybody was inside the house. Everybody heard him knock. Everybody sensed that there was something about their area of hurt, need, or desperation that they should open up to and develop. Everybody had felt the same pangs and desperation. Everybody had the same need and desire. Everyone was praying together in the house. So, when the vision came to that house, it came to all of them simultaneously. Yet only one lady got up and went to open the gate.

Some people may have been scared that it was late at night. Maybe they thought it was Herod's soldiers there to arrest another one of them. Some may have been sleeping. Some may have been too lazy to get up and open the gate. Some may have felt too big to go and get the gate. Some may have concluded that it was Rhoda's job to answer the door. All kinds of reasons may have been bandied around as to why they could not get up and open the gate. Many people received the vision, but only one person responded. As it happened in the days of Peter, so it does today.

For example, I have walked on filthy streets. I noticed that everyone was embarrassed by the trash. Because everyone passed by that way, everyone had the same nudge. Everybody wanted SOMEBODY to get the place cleaned up and beautify the place. The vision to start up a cleaning or beautification business visited everyone at the same time, just as Peter knocked on the general gate. In the same areas, people will complain about having no jobs.

Many people are in the same city with poor living conditions, human trafficking, bad roads, no electricity, no pipe-borne water, lack of basic amenities, poor leadership, injustice, racism, and wickedness all around. Everyone feels the pangs. But the majority of the people hide away out of fear or laziness or whatnot. Everyone feels the desire, but most people never recognise that this is a vision that they could explore.

When we see an invention, we only celebrate the name behind it. We think that the idea was unique to them. We say, "What a genius! He's very brilliant to have received that ground-breaking idea!"

Others might say, "He's so lucky. The universe aligned for him to discover that great principle."

But do you know that several other people, perhaps hundreds or thousands, or millions, may have caught the same vision? It only looks like only one or a few people caught the vision because most of those who caught the same vision did not act upon the idea they conceived. They suffered and ignored and managed the situation without making any difference in their world.

Many are so full of fear that they cannot wade into uncharted grounds. They prefer security over uncertainty, so they choose not to be pioneers. Some people cannot stand criticism, and so they let the pangs in their hearts die. A vast majority are just so lazy that they prefer the status quo.

You and I must have caught visions of marvellous things in the past, which we allowed our quaternions of fear, doubt, laziness, and vices, to kill. We must have heard the voice of great visions knocking upon the door of our hearts at some point. Had we implemented these things, we would have bettered our world. But unfortunately, we let these visions die, or we let others run with them instead.

One of my childhood friends told me his story which he has

permitted me to share. He said, "One evening, several years ago, after a game of football in your [the author's] neighbourhood, I was holding a small gas lighter in my hand and musing on it. I told my older brother, 'Can you imagine how someone has created a small device like this that can store enough energy to light bigger things? In the same way, we should be able to develop a portable device that stores power to charge our mobile phones without us connecting directly to an electric source.'"

My friend continued, "After that conversation, we went home, and completely forgot about that conversation for years. However, one day, I saw the mobile power bank which I had imagined years before. It dawned on me that I had imagined a useful invention that I never worked on. Someone else worked on it and pioneered it."

Like my friend, I have similar stories of imagined inventions which haunt me from time to time. You probably do too. We cannot keep giving excuses for ignoring or delaying the visions that God brings our way if we are serious about making an impact in this life.

I read a story about an aviation engineer who completed an airplane the year before the Wright brothers made the first flight of an airplane in Kitty Hawk, North Carolina. After building his plane, this engineer kept his invention in his barn, and never brought it to the public because he was afraid to fly it for whatever reason. Anyway, after hearing of Orville and Wilbur Wright's first successful flight, he then brought out his plane and flew it. Unfortunately, he has forever missed out on the opportunity to be called the pioneer of the airplane.

Some other people have been suggested as having developed or flown a plane before the Wright brothers, but they all did theirs clandestinely and off-the-record. Only Orville and Wilbur Wright were bold enough to gather everyone to come and watch their attempt to fly a plane. The first flight lasted only 12 seconds and detractors would have mocked them. But the failure made them improve the device. In the end, they pioneered the global aviation industry. Many people catch the same vision, but only those who bring it to manifestation get the praise if they see it through to the end.

LESSON 7: HEARKEN

*And as Peter knocked at the door of the gate, a
damsel came to hearken, named Rhoda.*

(Acts 12:13)

There is a vital place of stopping to hearken in the pursuit of your vision. Hearing is the point of filtering whether or not your vision is godly, decent, appropriate, accurate, just, sensible, realistic, and timely. When Peter knocked, Rhoda did not rush mindlessly to open the door for whoever or whatever was at the door. She went there to "hearken", that is, to "listen", "perceive", and "discern".

Why must you stop to hearken? Because just as there are good visions, there are also bad visions. You can catch a bad vision when you travail, just as you can catch a good vision. And people run with bad visions just as people run with good visions. For example, two women were born into average families in the same year. One of them decided to make her fame from helping the needy and sick people in society. The other dreamt of making her fame as a member of one of the most fearsome robbery gangs in American history. Each of them caught a vision, but while one caught a wholesome vision, the other caught an evil vision. The first was Mother Teresa, and the other was Bonnie Parker. Both of them were born in 1910. But while Mother Teresa was canonised for her devotion and humanitarian work, Bonnie Parker married fellow criminal, Clyde Chestnut Barrow, proudly lived for the devil, and will forever go down in the Hall of Infamy.

Behold, he <u>travaileth with iniquity</u>, and <u>hath conceived mischief</u>, and <u>brought forth falsehood</u>.

(Psalms 7:14)

This is why you should sit down and consider your vision from all angles. Does your vision align with God's Word? Did you catch your vision out of pride, envy, or competition? Are you desperate to prove yourself to people? Is this exactly what you should be pursuing at this time? Do not bring evil upon yourself and others by chasing an evil vision. Suppose Rhoda ran straight to open the door without listening to who was at the door, and it turned out to be armed robbers, the whole house would have been in trouble that night. You must gather all you can and learn all you can about the vision you carry.

Hearken to Discern Three Voices

(1) Hearken to discern God's voice: Search out His Word for His plans and promises. If you do not guide your vision according to God's Word, you will guide it according to the flesh or satanic plan. Once you have RIGHTLY divided the vision using the yardstick of God's Word, then you have completed the first part of hearkening. How do you hear God? First concentrate on studying, memorising, meditating on, and applying the Bible daily. You cannot hear God's voice when you do not pay attention to the Bible which is easily accessible to you. Afterward, pay attention to the ideas and noble deeds that are strongly impressed on your heart.

(2) Hearken to Experts' Opinions: They call them experts for a reason. While on your journey to your great vision, you cannot know all about it or do everything by yourself. You need to consult experts to guide you on some aspects. I do not mean that you take everything they say as gospel truth, but at least, listen to what they have to say.

As a master's student, I took a course entitled 'Environmental Impact Assessment'. Basically, it is about the different processes you must follow if you want to bring about any major change to an environment. You must consult very widely and carry out many studies. What is the safe way to go about this? What are the guiding laws and traditions of the land? What are current best practices? How can you improve the status quo? Whose permission do you need to start? How can you gather societal support? Where are the landmarks that you must never tamper with? Do you need to pay a commission or levy, and to whom? How does the plan affect plants and wildlife? What is the security situation in the area I want to work? These are examples of some of the questions that wise visionaries ask consultants.

In the process, you will be warned about some courses of action that you never considered on your own, and you will have to adjust accordingly. One way to crash very quickly is having no one to help and guide you. Listening to the right counsel is important. In the multitude of godly and sound counsellors, there is safety. Move with a team of like minds. You will enjoy more encouragement and strength than when you are isolated.

Where there is no counsel, the people fall: but in the multitude of counsellors there is safety.

Without counsel purposes are disappointed: but in the multitude of counsellors they are established.

(Proverbs 11:14; 15:22)

(3) Hearken to discern the voice of the wicked: In anticipation of your vision, you will be presented with offers to bribe you of our vision, counterfeit offers to scam you, robbers to steal your ideas, and saboteurs to destroy you from within. You must be perceptive to the infiltration of the enemy. Is this Satan? Is this a mistake? Am I off course? Rushing headlong in ignorance has caused the downfall of too many visionaries in history.

But while men slept, his enemy came and sowed tares among the wheat, and went his way.

(Matthew 13:25)

Many people have opened the door to the wrong things because they did not wait and listen. They were so desperate to have it here and now that they accepted anything that came their way. We should rather be like Rhoda. Take a moment to listen and evaluate before opening the door to the ideas knocking on the door of your heart.

LESSON 8: WHOEVER FIRST PURSUES THE VISION MATTERS A LOT

And as Peter knocked at the door of the gate, a damsel came to hearken, named Rhoda.

(Acts 12:13)

Many times, the one who first decides to run with the vision determines to a very large extent, the direction and outcome of the idea. The way they interpret the vision, relay it to others, and direct its actualisation, determines how close what we get is to the original vision that was caught.

In Peter's case, a damsel called Rhoda was the first person to acknowledge the vision and welcome it when it knocked on the door. So many good visions have been corrupted because of the whims and caprices of the one who called the shots. Moreover, deciding to run with a vision is no guarantee that the vision will be actualised if the person who decides to bring it to pass does not go about it the right way.

Rhoda could easily have told those inside that it was an intruder, an impostor, or a ghost at the door. She could have asked Peter to get lost. How many people will you open the door to in the dead of the night? It will be weirder if they are impersonating your loved one who was jailed. It makes no sense. But thank God for Rhoda's personality. She had an open, exploratory heart to believe the impossible. Her role was pivotal in the outcome of this story.

Seven Personality Traits to Imbibe from Rhoda

(1) Rhoda had a young heart:

And as Peter knocked at the door of the gate, <u>a damsel came to hearken</u>, named Rhoda.

(Acts 12:13)

"Damsel" means "a young unmarried woman". A young person is usually exploratory and adventurous. It is uncommon to see a man of 80 years old seeking an exciting new adventure or trying to build the latest invention. Young people see visions more commonly than old people, while old people usually dream dreams (Joel 2:28).

And it shall come to pass afterward, that I will pour out my spirit upon all flesh; and your sons and your daughters shall prophesy, your old men shall dream dreams, your young men shall see visions:

(Joel 2:28)

While you can run with a vision, a dream is normally a long-term vision that may not be accomplished within a short time, maybe even in your lifetime. Martin Luther King (Jr.) said, "I have a dream...!" but he never lived to see it. Rhoda's damsel heart was unclouded by people shouting, "You cannot do that! That is impossible! Stop that! Drop that! Quit that!" Her mind was unspoiled.

It is not a rule, but to bring a vision to pass, being a youth is an added advantage. A youth is older and more mature than a child but also presumably has some extra time on their hands than the aged, to bring a vision to pass in their lifetime. An old man is aware that his time will soon be up. He is trying to wrap up his assignment and put his house in order. But no matter your age, if you have a "damsel" heart (young, teachable, and excited mind of possibilities like Rhoda) you can still pursue the impossible. You can still be hungry to see the imaginations in your head manifest in your hands. Rhoda being young highlights the importance of being timely, flexible, teachable, and strong, in bringing your vision to pass.

(2) Rhoda was focused: Being unmarried in the context of your vision symbolises a person who is completely focused. In I Corinthians 7:34, we are told that a married woman is distracted by things of this world while a single woman or damsel fully focuses on things of God, such as a God-given vision. Unmarried people in this context, therefore, represent those who have cut off all distractions to focus solely on the vision.

There is difference also between a wife and a virgin [a damsel, an unmarried person]. *The unmarried woman careth for the things of the Lord... but she that is married careth for the things of the world* [or is distracted], *how she may please her husband.*

(I Corinthians 7:34)

I am not saying that you should not get married (although marriage is an excuse some people give for not pursuing their vision). I am only drawing parallels. In the pursuit of your vision, quit wasting time on irrelevant things. Unprofitable people, places, and things should be cut off from your life to free up time, energy, and resources for your vision. That is what being single here is all about. In this day and age, millions of people are married to social media. It has made them superficial attention-seekers who cannot stay off the limelight to build a lasting legacy. Free yourself from distractions like Rhoda.

(3) Rhoda was humble: Bear in mind that at the time that Rhoda went to get the door alone, no one knew that Peter was knocking. Rhoda was fine with doing a thankless job alone with no one cheering, funding, or supporting her. In the process, she encountered the answer to her prayers.

A man's pride shall bring him low: but honour shall uphold the humble in spirit.

(Proverbs 29:23)

Do not be like the majority of people who refuse to go the extra mile in their line of service. They insist on contributing only to the extent of their wages or salary. Some others will never do a job they consider as not matching their status. These people commonly remain at the same level for a long, long time. It is when you showcase your expertise cheaply at first that people notice what you can do and they tell others. Zig Ziglar said, "When you do more than you are paid for, you will eventually be paid for more than you do." Rhoda's humility and readiness to do the thankless job brought her in contact with the vision.

(4) Rhoda was a woman of the Word and prayer: Rhoda could have been in her house sleeping. Instead, she was at a prayer vigil to see her vision through. She conceived the vision. Then she fought physically and spiritually to disband the quaternions of soldiers around her vision.

In addition to prayer, being glad over something that you believe in your heart but have not seen with your eyes is a hallmark of faith. When she heard Peter's voice, she believed at once in the improbable possibility that Peter was there. She never doubted it once, but received with gladness that it was ready to manifest. She was so glad that the joy momentarily paralysed her! That's faith!

And when she knew Peter's voice, <u>she opened not the gate</u> for <u>gladness</u>...

(Acts 12:14)

Without seeing him, she believed it was Peter, the substance of things hoped for. Studying and meditating on God's Word is the Bible-prescribed way to build up your faith. Her faith came from soaking in the Word of God (Romans 10:17). Hence, Rhoda took the Word seriously until it infused the possibility mentality into her.

Now faith is the substance of things hoped for, the evidence of things not seen.

(Hebrews 11:1)

(5) Rhoda was committed to self-development:

And when she knew Peter's voice...

(Acts 12:14)

How did Rhoda KNOW Peter's voice? She must have fellowshipped with the vision long enough to know what he looked and sounded like. There might have been some people in that house who were praying for Peter who did not even know what he looked or sounded like. If one of them had gone to answer the door, he would have heard the voice of a stranger and sent him away. That would have been the end of the vision. But Rhoda had seen Peter, heard him speak, read his writings, and known him up close to the point of recognising his muffled voice behind a door. In the course of pursuing your vision, you must gather enough information about what you want to do. You must read studiously in line with what you want to actualise.

When a person tells me any project they want to embark upon, the first thing I tell them is, "Study as much as you can about it." Most think it's not necessary. "Since God said it, it will surely happen. I'm a Christian. That cannot happen to me." Then they try to freestyle their way to success. They soon learn in the school of hard knocks that to succeed, ignorance is costlier than knowledge with planning. Having faith is no substitute to getting practical and taking the right steps. Even if the vision succeeds, it may not grow to the scale that it should, because you lack a lot of fundamental information. Wisdom, knowledge, and understanding gathered from studying will never be overlooked on the way to succeeding in your vision.

(6) Rhoda was a great team player: Rhoda could have opened the door to Peter and claimed the glory for herself. Instead, she recognised that the whole team had prayed together and contributed towards bringing him back. She ran in and informed them so that everybody could be part of the welcoming party before she opened the door. She was not interested in being the star of the show. What an amazing personality! Don't be about taking the credit and hugging the spotlight. Recognise everyone who played a part in bringing the vision to pass and give them due credit.

And when she knew Peter's voice, she opened not the gate for gladness, but ran in, and told how Peter stood before the gate.

(Acts 12:14)

(7) Rhoda's name suggests that she didn't give excuses: The name "Rhoda" means "rose". A rose plant is full of prickles (thorny protrusions) all over. But at the end of the plant comes very beautiful roses. A rose, therefore, is something beautiful that rises out of difficult situations. A rose does not blame its difficult background or sad past as the reason it does not manifest its potential. It does not clam up and say that prickles will impale its petals. It does not resign to the fact that its petals were pricked last week. A rose plant just keeps growing to the point where it flowers beautifully at the end.

From her name and personality, it comes right at us that Rhoda was not one given to excuses. She did not blame her parents' divorce, childhood poverty, her age, skin colour, or nationality, as why she will not see her vision through. She did not refuse an education because she was already 30 and will be sitting among kids in high school. Rhoda's name, "rose", suggests that she was someone who ran with the vision no matter the difficulties and disadvantages around her. Despite all the persecution she went through as a member of the Church, she got up, went up to the vision, heard its voice, and believed with gladness.

Those who are given to excuses can never obtain the vision. It does not matter that our potentials are great. It does not matter that God loves you very much. It does not matter how connected you are. Once you are one given to excuses, God cannot do much with you. In Jesus' parable in Luke 14:16-24, a wealthy man made a great feast. After inviting family, friends, and noblemen in society, they came up with one excuse after another to not attend the feast. This wealthy man got angry and discarded them all! He sent his servant to invite all the poor and forgotten people on the streets and in the creeks. He ran his vision with nobodies and nonentities because they did not give excuses. A talented and favoured man that is given to excuses is of limited usefulness in God's hands. On the contrary, a nobody that is available to God and ready to work will be used and promoted because he will not give excuses to exempt himself.

LESSON 9: THE VISION EXCITES YOU SO MUCH, BUT...!

And when she knew Peter's voice, she opened not the gate for gladness, but ran in, and told how Peter stood before the gate. And they said unto her, Thou art mad...

(Acts 12:14-15)

When you catch a great vision, you get super excited! It lights you up so much that it becomes all you think about throughout the day. You draw up plans, permutations, and budgets. You can't wait to get started! And because the excitement and positivity in you are so much, you badly want to share the vision with anyone at the slightest opportunity. Typically, these will be your loved ones. Rhoda was no different. She was so numb with excitement that she could not simply open the gate to Peter. She first ran in to share the super-exciting news.

And when she knew Peter's voice, she opened not the gate for gladness, but ran in, and told how Peter stood before the gate...

(Acts 12:14)

This great idea is capable of causing a big positive change! It will bring you fulfilment! It will transform lives for the better. It will shoot you into the limelight! That great plan will end your family's generational poverty. They will certainly benefit from it when it is done. It's a no-brainer—they will certainly support it! Where is the logic in not supporting you?

And then Rhoda realised the bitter truth—nothing creates sworn haters like having a big vision! Your listeners will be completely indifferent to your news. They will say, "That's impossible! You're crazy! You're in way over your head, and you must kill such a senseless idea." Get prepared for that! There has never been any great man or woman who walked the face of the earth whose enemies did not multiply when they caught a vision.

And they said unto her, Thou art mad...

(Acts 12:15)

You are confused. You don't understand! What happens is that their mental capacity has not expanded enough to accommodate such a big idea and it appears impossible to them. They cannot see it happening. A lot of people talk big, daydream, and wish for big things. But when it boils down to it, when it comes to believing in your heart and pursuing, you will be on your own just like Rhoda. They think it is too big to ever be accomplished. Hence, they will attempt to shrink you to the size of their fear by asking you to abandon it. For others, you are attempting to disrupt the status quo which they are so comfortable with, and for that, they will fight you with their last blood to protect the little territory they have. Otherwise, it may simply be out of envy.

The Fight from Within Will be the Fiercest!

What hurts the most is that majority of those who oppose the idea at the early stage will be those that you hold very dear to you. They may include your parents, siblings, spouse, friends, teachers, students, mentors, role models, colleagues, co-workers, bosses, employees, associates, and others in your close circles who hear about the vision. These are people whose love, support, and encouragement mean a lot to you. You want them to make you feel like you are part of the family. You anticipate that their excitement and motivation will be the needed boost in the pursuit of your target. Maybe you expect them to contribute their own effort and resources towards the project. You are hurt and confused when they reject "your crazy plan."

If you are among the very few visioners on earth to have other visionaries in their circle, then you may have a few supporters at the beginning. But either way, it is always a few people or no one at all initially. Prepare to be your only cheerleader at the start of the race. It will minimise your heartache. The journey will be demanding. Adding unmet expectations to it will be a hefty weight that may crush you. The bigger your vision and the fewer visionaries are in your circle, the more likely, and the fiercer, you will be opposed.

There will always be haters, competitors, and workers of darkness outside your fold who will fight you. But I tell you with all certainty that the combined efforts of all your external enemies is child's play compared to the stiff opposition you will encounter from within.

And a man's foes shall be they of his own household.

(Matthew 10:36)

Ask Joseph. His family fought his vision harder than any other force in his life. His brothers plotted to kill him because of his dreams. They dumped him in an empty pit. The fall could have broken his limbs. Finally, they sold him into slavery so he will have no chance to actualise his vision of greatness. If God had not intervened, his vision would have been aborted before it ever started.

...And they hated him yet the more <u>for his dreams, and for his words</u>. And they said to one another, Behold, this dreamer cometh. Come now therefore, and let us slay him, and cast him into some pit...<u>and we will see what will become of his dreams</u>.

(Genesis 37:8,19-20)

When you think of Samson, Delilah comes to mind. But before Delilah betrayed him, he had a remarkable experience in this regard. In the days of Samson, the Israelites were under tribute to the Philistines because of their sin (Judges 13:1). Finally, God had mercy on them and sent Samson as their deliverer (Judges 13). Samson made life miserable for the Philistines (Judges 14-15). They tried everything they could to capture him or kill him but God protected him.

But while everyone else saw Samson as a powerful deliverer with a vision to deliver Israel from Philistine bondage, his tribesmen, the men of Judah, saw him as an ordinary troublemaker, a street urchin, or riffraff. They said among themselves, "Let us get rid of this troublemaker once and for all. He's a nuisance and could get us into trouble."

Then three thousand of his tribesmen went to capture him and handed him over to the Philistines. The Philistines never even asked them for such a favour. They just could not afford to be disliked by their taskmasters because of an ordinary rabble-rouser. They were too scared to think of his vision of national independence. Therefore, it was either he constricted his vision to the level of their fear, or...! They were his kinsmen.

Then three thousand men of Judah...said to Samson, Knowest thou not that the Philistines are rulers over us? what is this that thou hast done unto us?... And they said unto him, We are come down to bind thee, that we may deliver thee into the hand of the Philistines... And they bound him with two new cords, and brought him up from the rock.

(Judges 15:11-13)

When Goliath scoffed at Israel, no one in Israel had the faith or might to confront him. But when David saw Goliath, he caught a vision of bringing him down and saving his nation. The first antagonist of his vision was his oldest brother (I Samuel 17:26-28). He never saw a national deliverer in David. He only saw his little shepherd brother. It is common for you to be celebrated in public but not mean much to your household.

Those in Jesus' hometown looked down on Him and were offended that He started His ministry. They shunned His meetings and received the least impartation from his ministry. The surprising this was that even the Pharisees that hated Jesus attended His meetings regularly and asked Him many questions. But His own kinsmen did not think He was that important for them to attend His meetings.

I imagine two people having a side-talk about Him. One says,

"Who does this guy think he is?! What has come over him?! We know Him. He's that carpenter guy that lives three streets from Capernaum market. I even heard from reliable sources that he's not the biological son of the man he calls his dad. They say he's a bastard that was foisted on the man."

"You mean it?!" replied the other. "I know him well. He came to fix our roof before. I know he never got beyond primary education. How did he learn all these things he's teaching? This stuff is clearly beyond his league."

"True. And what right has he to teach in the synagogue anyway? He is neither a Levite nor has he any formal Bible training. They should put away this crazy attention-seeker for good!"

"I second that. We've had enough of his heresies!"

And he went out from there, and came into his own country; and his disciples follow him.

And when the Sabbath day was come, he began to teach in the synagogue: and many hearing him were astonished, saying, From where has this man these things? and what wisdom is this which is given to him, that even such mighty works are performed by his hands?

Is not this the carpenter, the son of Mary, the brother of James, and Joses, and of Juda, and Simon? and are his sisters not here with us? And they were offended at him.

But Jesus, said unto them, A prophet is not without honour, but in his own country, and among his own kin, and in his own house.

And he could there do no mighty work, save that he laid his hands upon a few sick folk, and healed them.

(Mark 6:1-5)

And their unbelief incapacitated His anointing. 'The Message' Bible says that He did not do many miracles there '*because of their hostile indifference*'. That's what we're talking about!

Expect them to convince others to take sides with them to hate you. You will receive phone calls and meeting invitations to straighten you out. Petitions will be written against you. Your idea will be ridiculed, your equipment destroyed, and you will probably be physically attacked. Paul's dream of spreading the gospel of Jesus to people who were not Jews got him into a lot of hot water. He was arrested, beaten, jailed, summoned, ostracised, ridiculed, and stoned. At the height of it, his former colleagues took an oath to kill him because of his vision of enlightening the Gentiles the with Good News. Too many visioners have been killed. It's a risky business and no wonder many are scared off.

And when it was day, certain of the Jews banded together, and bound themselves under a curse, saying that they would neither eat nor drink till they had killed Paul.

(Acts 23:12)

The pain, shame, and disappointment associated with this phase are so great that only the strong will survive it, often with lots of tears and scars. If the fire burning you comes from outside your camp, the encouragement of your loved ones can help you feel better throughout the process. But if the fire burning you comes from within your camp, from people you just cannot break away from, then life becomes a living hell! After a long and stressful day of making little or no progress in your labour, you will not even want to return home to rest. You are *persona non grata* in your home or group; the black sheep of the family; the nutcase that everyone avoids. Why? "You must abandon your dream!"

As this is the toughest phase of actualising your vision, it is the single biggest cemetery of most talents and visions. Only a few strong people scale through to the other side. At this critical point, you often MUST choose between your vision and your loved ones who are unsupportive and mad at you. Most visioners chicken out here. They forfeit their vision because they place the validation of their family and friends above the vision. They can't manage the loneliness and isolation that comes with being the odd one out.

You must be tough. Tough men are men who endure tough times.

Tough times may last long, but tough people last longer. Develop a thick skin to hatred, criticism, and ostracisation if you want to go far in life.

If your vision scales through this phase of stiff opposition, the most difficult part is over. If you successfully win some over with your persistence, then your vision has a big chance of materialising. Remember, it is not going to be easy, and the time required to overcome differs for each individual and scenario. It may be a few days for some fortunate individuals, and decades or a lifetime (or never!) for others.

Maybe you are already at that phase and are about to give up, or you already quit because it was unbearable. Or maybe you felt you were alone in being ostracised. Every great man had his own similar experience, and this book will have no end if we include everyone's story. Perhaps you have already been there and you excelled. I congratulate you. I am sure you agree that this point is extremely challenging.

Rhoda could not understand being called a mad girl. It was not the excitement that she anticipated from her church members. They were the same people who smiled at her and called her "Sister Rhoda" at Sunday services. They were the same people she had teamed up with to pray for Peter. They were the same people who commended her humility and hospitality. And yet, when she decided to achieve beyond the status quo, they immediately turned on her viciously like a pack of wolves. "You must be out of your mind! How dare you come up with such a ridiculous idea?!" She was shocked, embarrassed, and confused. Prepare for it because you will definitely go through it on your way to actualising your vision.

We must draw a line here. You need people in your camp to tell you the truth and bring you back to earth if you are in pursuit of vanity. Your family is not necessarily against you just because they disagree with your plans. For instance, you cannot take all the family's emergency savings and children's school fees and blow it all up on what you call a vision. You must be guided by wisdom and consideration for others. Be sure your vision is backed by the Word of God and executed with divine wisdom and circumspectness.

LESSON 10: KEEP AFFIRMING YOUR VISION CONSTANTLY

And they said unto her, Thou art mad. <u>But she constantly affirmed that it was even so</u>…

(Acts 12:15)

Rhoda was not one to let criticism shut her up, not even if it came from her church. She CONSTANTLY affirmed her vision to herself and others. To be "constant" is to remain the same or maintain a position, even if all hell is let loose or the sky falls down. It also hints at being frequent at something. Rhoda affirmed her vision constantly in the face of all opposition. She did not care who believed her and who did not. She was sure of the vision she had caught, and she was going to stand by it no matter the opposition. We need to stop being addicted to human affirmation and focus solely on God's Word. You will never do anything meaningful with your life if you crave human validation. You will never serve God and never pursue greatness. Serving God and pursuing greatness draw severe criticism when you decide to get serious.

As we have read, the criticism can even come from the Church. In the recent past (and some Christian denominations still teach that), the Church believed that the power of God was done away with when the last apostle died. The prevailing doctrine was that healing, deliverance, breakthroughs, and all-round blessings had been done away with. Many of the men who caught the revelation of the full Gospel which we enjoy today, encountered stiff opposition, including from their churches and households. Today, we believe the full Gospel doctrine because we were probably born into a church that teaches it or we heard it early on in our walk with God. But the fathers laboured to get us here.

Andrew Wommack started studying the Bible for himself at a young age. He began discovering truths of our redemptive rights for himself. He caught a vision of living and teaching a full Gospel message. When his Baptist church found out about his new doctrine, he was thrown out of the church and uninvited. Yet he continued to teach and abide by the revelation he caught. Today, his ministry has blessed millions of people across the globe. Men like that who affirm and continue through the criticism are those who make real impact. They are not scared to be pioneers of the vision they carry. They are not afraid of rejection. If they stopped affirming their conviction, it would have been over before it all started.

In defending your vision, nothing can overcome well-rooted Word of God. Familiarise yourself with verses of Scripture that affirm God's unlimited ability (such as Genesis 18:14, Matthew 19:26, Mark 10:27, Luke 1:37, and Luke 18:27). Feed yourself CONSTANTLY like Rhoda. It is the Word of God that builds your faith (Romans 10:17). So, get stuffed with it. To get stuffed is to be full and puffy with something. Look at a teddy bear. We call it a stuffed toy. It is full of foam to the point that it is puffy. Get stuffed with the Word like that. It is what you are stuffed with that comes out of you when you speak.

When someone says, "It is impossible," reply them with what God's Word says about impossibility. We do not operate by human strength but by divine empowerment.

Tell them, "I'm not banking on my own ability to accomplish this but through the Holy Spirit's empowerment." (Zechariah 4:6). Remind them, "For me, it is impossible. But with God, nothing is impossible. And God is with me on this (and please be sure that it is not a whimsical, selfish, or nonsensical ambition that you call a vision).

If they say, "You're crazy/weird," tell them, "I'm not crazy/ weird, I'm just different." Remember, the man in Christ thinks differently. God gives you a different mindset to the old you when you are in Jesus (II Corinthians 5:17; II Timothy 1:7). Tell them, "We are all different. We can't all be the same. You are different from me and I am different from you. We shouldn't quarrel over that. Variety is the spice of life."

Someone will remark very candidly, "You just can't pull this off! It's too big!"

"I can do all things through Christ who strengthens me!" (Philippians 4:13). If man could land on the moon, then this is possible. Be enthusiastic about your vision and tell doubters with all confidence how much you believe in the dream. Remember, at some point, you will be your only cheerleader. If you stop cheering for yourself, you will not be cheered. It's that simple.

Make your doubters understand that if it fails, your spirit will not be dampened. "If I fail, I would have gained some knowledge and experience along the way. Let me enjoy the adventure." "If I embark on it, I MAY succeed. But if I never try, I am already guaranteed to fail. Let me take my chance."

More than you tell others, speak to yourself. Remind yourself that it is possible. Every opportunity to see yourself in the mirror should be another opportunity to imagine yourself as what you will look like when the vision is accomplished.

Why am I emphasising the use of words? Because words are your greatest weapon. They determine to a great extent whether you win or lose. There was nothing that God created without speaking words. Why should it be different for you?

And God said, Let there be light: and there was light.

(Genesis 1:3)

Death and life are in the power of the tongue, and they that love it shall eat the fruit thereof.

(Proverbs 18:21)

David was a man who understood how powerful words are. Right from the moment he saw Goliath, he started speaking words of faith. He asked the guards, "Who is this uncircumcised Philistine defying the army of the living God? What will they give the man who kills him?" (I Samuel 17:26). The guards told him. Then his older brother came and rebuked him for having a vision of killing Goliath. He replied, "What have I done? Is it not a valid vision to see God's army delivered?" (I Samuel 17:29).

David kept speaking until they brought him before King Saul. When Saul doubted his ability, he spoke more words of faith. He told Saul, "Because this man has defied the army of the living God, I have caught a vision to kill him like the lion and the bear that I killed. And he is going down today!" (I Samuel 17:36). Words! David went on to affirm that he was not relying on his own strength but on the help of God. That's the right approach. I can do it through Christ that strengthens me.

Finally, David came face-to-face with Goliath and Goliath boasted and threatened. Again, David started speaking heavy-duty faith-packed words against his problem. David knew that the Philistine was big and powerful. The only advantage he had over Goliath was that he could speak powerful words.

Then said David to the Philistine, You come to me with a sword, and with a spear, and with a shield: but I come to you in the name of the LORD of hosts, the God of the armies of Israel whom you have defied.

This day will the LORD deliver you into my hand; and I will smite you, and take your head from you; and I will give the carcasses of the host of the Philistines this day to the fowls of the air, and to the wild beasts of the earth; that all earth may know that there is a God in Israel.

(I Samuel 17:45-46)

That was where David won the battle. Nothing could stand against those explosive words! The demons driving Goliath ran for cover in the nearby bushes when they heard the words of faith. Those words paralysed Goliath when the stone came flying at his head because by not countering them, he had agreed to them and they were established. Goliath saw David swinging the sling. He knew what was he was about to do. He saw the stone coming and could have turned his head to one side even so slightly and the stone would have hit his helmet. But he was arrested on the spot by the spoken Word. Affirming his vision worked for David. It worked for Jesus. It will work for you. Don't be convinced it can be done without CONSTANT use of words like Rhoda. Seeing is never enough. You must also speak it!

The Place of Writing

Apart from speaking, ensure to WRITE down the vision. That way, you can remember all aspects of it. You can keep track of your progress. You can read it out loud often without missing any aspect. And you can send it to others who can help you run with it while you are there and when you are gone. Writing is important.

Solomon did not catch the vision of building God's temple— David did. There was absolutely no way that Solomon would have built exactly the same structure that David had in mind. Yet Solomon did. How was it possible? You see, when David caught the revelation of the temple, the Bible says that he wrote every detail and pattern down and handed them to Solomon in a private ceremony. By reading the patterns and documents from his father, Solomon had specific guidelines for the construction of the temple. These specifications guided him even after the death of his father. By writing the vision, David had preserved its exactness so that his successor would continue his vision. And the Bible says that they build EXACTLY what David had in mind. This happened because he wrote down his vision. This is a major benefit of writing.

11 Then David gave to Solomon his son the pattern of the porch, and of the houses thereof, and of the treasuries thereof, and of the upper chambers thereof, and of the inner parlours thereof, and of the place of the mercy seat,

12 And the pattern of all that he had by the spirit, of the courts of the house of the LORD, and of all the chambers round about, of the treasuries of the house of God, and of the treasuries of the dedicated things:

13 Also for the courses of the priests and the Levites, and for all the work of the service of the house of the LORD, and for all the vessels of service in the house of the LORD.

19 All this, said David, <u>the LORD made me understand in writing by his hand upon me</u>, even all the works of this pattern.

(I Chronicles 28:11)

Are you writing down your vision? Or are you just depending on your memory? Any vision that must survive to the next generation must be documented. If it is not, every new captain in the ship will drive it in a different direction time. Are you a businessman, a leader, or just an individual? Write down your vision. Write down what you stand for. Write down what your organisation stands for and where you are headed.

I once watched a whispering game, and you can try it too. In the game, you line up about a dozen people in a row. Then you whisper some information into the ear of the first person on the row. The first person whispers the message into the ear of the second person on the row. The second person whispers the message to the third, and on and on until the penultimate person whispers the message into the ear of the last person. Then the last person says the message out loud. Invariably, the message the last person says is VERY different from what the initial person said. Down the line, some part of the message will have been omitted, rephrased, forgotten, and added to, until you could barely recognise the original message.

But if you write the same message on a piece of paper and ask them to read and pass the paper down the line, the same message is passed down from the first person on the row to the last person. That tells you that writing preserves the exactness of the vision, no matter how many people receive the message.

The Bible is an example of a vision written down. Now we have as close as possible to God's original message because we depend on the written transmission, not on verbal transmission. There are books and journals written by men like John Wesley and Isaac Newton stored in special archives. We know exactly what they said or did because they wrote them for us to read. If their exploits were passed down the generations, we will never have gotten the exact information. That is what births myths, legends, and traditional folk tales that are inaccurate, warped, exaggerated, and unbelievable.

And the LORD answered me, and said, <u>Write the vision, and make it plain on tables</u>, that he may run that reads it.

(Habakkuk 2:2)

Writing down your vision is God's prescription for letting others run with them in the exact form that you have in mind. Write your business plan. Write your ideas and goals. Write down the inventions in your head. God asked you to. Leave it in places where you can easily refer to them. You will be glad you obeyed God.

I watched Steve Harvey's video in which he narrated how his teacher ran him down with words. When he was in sixth grade, his teacher gave the class an assignment to write what they wanted to be in the future. Steve Harvey wrote in his assignment that he wanted to be on TV in the future. When the teacher read it, she was angry. She called him to the front of the class and openly ridiculed him. She said that Steve, who was a stammerer at the time, will never appear on TV. She called his parents and reported to them that Steve was trying to be a Smart Alec.

When Steve got home, his parents confronted him over the essay. His mother said, "Slick [his dad's name], your son is being a Smart Alec at school. He wrote in his essay that he wants to appear on TV." Steve said he knew already that he was going to get whipped for "offending".

To his surprise, his father said, "What's wrong with wanting to be on TV?"

His mother replied, "His being a Smart Alec and writing something unbelievable on his paper!"

Steve's father differed. He said, "How come the boy cannot write that he wants to be on TV?"

This caused his dad and mum to start an argument and they sent him into his room. His mother sided with the teacher while his father saw nothing wrong with his vision of wanting to be on TV.

While he was still expecting to be whipped, his father entered his room. He asked Steve, "What did she want you to put on your paper?"

Steve answered, "Well, I don't know, Daddy. Maybe a basketball player, or something like what all the other kids wrote."

Steve's dad advised, "Well, put what she wants on a paper. Take it to school tomorrow and give it to her. Take your paper [with your vision] and put it in your drawer. Every morning when you get up, read your paper. And every night before you get to bed, read your paper."

Steve obeyed. In the process, he realised through his father's advice the importance of speaking the vision, writing it down, and referring to it constantly. Today, Steve Harvey is a Christian and a worldwide name in the world of entertainment.

Affirm your vision with words and write them. Keep reading and speaking it in the face of doubt, unbelief, and difficulties. When you affirm your vision enough, it becomes firm in your heart. And with the words spoken, forces begin to move about to bring about your words. Writing helps you preserve it outside of your mind. It helps you read it as often as you want and get convinced of it. It is also a way that those coming after can refer to the original idea and not deviate from it.

Remove not the ancient landmark, which your fathers have set.

(Proverbs 22:28)

The ancient landmarks being referred to are guidelines for godly living given to the Israelites to follow. How could the children of Israel have known the "ancient landmark" if they had no official document to refer back to and guide their actions? The information was documented, and they constantly referred to it and observed it. As powerful as God's Word is, if it was not written down, it will never have survived up till now. Don't be reluctant to write down the vision that God gave you.

LESSON 11: PEOPLE WILL SUGGEST SMALLER ALTERNATIVES AND OTHER POSSIBILITIES

...But she constantly affirmed that it was even so. <u>Then said they, It is his angel</u>.

(Acts 12:15)

When Rhoda refused to back down, those inside the house started to see some light in her affirmation. Little by little, their mental capacity started expanding to the possibility that something LIKE THAT (but not that exactly) may be possible. They insisted that although Peter could not be at the door, maybe his angel was. Maybe they agreed with her just to shut her up.

What is your 'Peter's Angel'? It represents something related or similar to your vision but not exactly your vision. It is a downgrade, parody, or caricature of what you imagine. They will advise you, "You cannot create a spaceship that will land on Mars. But you may create a satellite that will orbit the earth. THAT'S possible."

Sometimes, they will make spiteful jokes about your vision. They will call it funny names. Saying, "It is his angel," may be a way of mocking Rhoda. Although some may have meant it, others may have been mocking her. Remember, an angel is a spirit. It has no physical substance. An angel does not come in and live with you. It delivers a message and leaves very quickly. Calling your vision an angel is to say that it lacks the substance to make it last and that the impact, if any, will be fleeting.

Sometimes, your loved ones will see the pain you are going through in trying to achieve the impossible. Out of pity for you, they will suggest a way out. "Why do you still want to accomplish _____? You should quit and do _____ instead." But nothing good comes easy.

What should you do when people suggest downgrades and caricatures of your vision? Do not downgrade the vision to their expectations. If someone else rises to the challenge and executes the vision despite their criticism, these same people will praise the other person for achieving the impossible and spite you for being unable to finish what you started. If you try and fail, you will be a laughingstock. If you stop along the line, you will equally be a laughingstock. Either way, mockers will mock. Pursue the vision then, you just might attain it. If you fail, you will be wiser.

Those who live by man's validation end up biting their fingers. Do not make that mistake! King Saul made the mistake. Before Goliath came on the scene, King Saul had fought and won some great battles. That should have built up his faith in God. He should have realised that safety is of the Lord. Instead, when Goliath came, he ran inside in fear. He felt the pang of the giant's defiance. He wanted Goliath dead. But instead of operating by faith, he listened to whispers of fear among his advisers. "That man is a champion." "The giant is big!" So, he chickened out of battle, clammed up in his tent, and killed the vision.

When David heard the same words about Goliath, his faith stood strong. He went out and killed Goliath in spite of the discouragement. When he returned, the same Israelites who said, "Don't go out there, the giant is mighty!" were the same ones who said, "Saul has killed **thousands**, and David has killed **tens of thousands**." They put David above the king.

Had David killed tens of thousands of Philistines? No! At this point, he had only killed ONE Philistine, and that was Goliath. On the contrary, Saul had actually killed tens of thousands of Philistines in battle. But they ridiculed Saul because he was afraid of facing Goliath. That is what happens when you listen to the voice of discouragers. It is a lose-lose situation with them, so why give up your dream for them?!

And it came to pass as they came, when David was returned from the slaughter of the Philistine, that the women came out of all cities of Israel, singing and dancing, to meet king Saul, with tabrets, with joy, and with instruments of music.

And the women answered one another as they played, and said, Saul has slain his thousands, and David his ten thousands.

(I Samuel 18:6-7)

Saul became furious when he heard the song (I Samuel 18:8). He developed envy toward David and tried to kill him. If only he had introspected, he would have realised that he was humiliated for giving in to fear and alternatives. Stay strong in faith and conviction. Do not accept a downgrade.

LESSON 12: WHEN YOUR VISION BECOMES SUCCESSFUL, EVERYONE WILL ASSOCIATE WITH IT

*But Peter continued knocking: and when **THEY** had opened the door, and saw him, they were astonished.*

(Acts 12:16)

Finally, someone said, "Let's go and open the door to prove that she has gone mental."

Another said, "Let's go and see the angel at the door [the nonsense/phantom she has been building]."

Yet another suggested, "Let's go and see what she's talking about."

So, some of them who cared got up and stood behind the door.

Someone asked, "Who is that?"

Peter replied in a quiet tone, "It's me."

"You who?"

"Peter."

"Peter who?"

"Peter...Simon Peter. Please open the door!"

They began exchanging glances and making all kinds of comments. "That's Peter's voice!" "Simon what?" "Spooky!" "Unbelievable!"

Elder Johnson quieted the group, "Sshh! Let me hear clearly!"

Peter whispered, getting exasperated, "Elder Johnson, are you going to open the door, or will you let the night guards re-arrest me?! And it's cold out here!"

Suddenly, they all realised that it was really Peter. An angel cannot feel cold or get arrested. And that was unmistakably Peter's voice. They exchanged wide-eyed glances. Rhoda was right after all! It was THE vision. The one they called impossible. The one they fought so hard to discredit and kill.

Instantly, the mood in the house transformed from gloom and doubt to immense joy! It was a triumphant, historic moment of glory for the Church! In an instant, they forgot about how they called Rhoda a mad girl. They never mentioned how they made jokes about her hallucinating and hearing a ghost. They forgot the alternatives they suggested to her. They forgot the stiff opposition and roadblocks they cast in the way of her vision. Rhoda herself was forgotten and no longer mentioned in the rest of the story. Those who initially opposed her flung themselves into the picture and blurred her out. They all gathered at the door. At the moment of glory, Rhoda was no longer alone.

*...and when **THEY** had opened the door...*

(Acts 12:16)

The Bible says that "they", not "she", opened the door for him at the moment of success. Who and who comprised the "they" that opened the door at the project's commissioning ceremony? "They" included those who were fast asleep when the vision came. "They" included those who sat down and ignored the vision when Peter knocked. "They" included those who opposed Rhoda and called her a mad girl for suggesting that Peter was at the door. "They" included those who suggested alternatives and other rational explanations. They all came to claim a part of the miracle.

Such is life. When your vision becomes successful, expect it to happen to you. Everyone will associate with your success. They will tell how they contributed in one way or another. Those who told you that you can never amount to anything will jostle for a front seat when you are to receive a gold medal. They will find a way to bring themselves into your success story—in a positive light, of course! They will tell you how they "pushed" you to achieve your highest potential. Even a person who just casually waved a greeting at you will analyse in detail how their greeting brought about your success. Success has many friends. Failure is an orphan. But you must be loyal and give due credit to those people who were actually present on the dark and lonely nights.

When she turned out to be right, Rhoda did not chastise all those who fought her. She did not call out all the deacons that doubted her vision and sanity and give them a reciprocal tongue-lashing. Achieving the vision is enough revenge against those who disbelieved it but now want to be part of it. Deep down in their hearts, they know what they did. Some of them will apologise, but most never will. Be ready to forgive and move on from those who insulted and criticised you who now want to associate with the vision that has manifested.

As Prime minister, Joseph did not execute his brothers for the evil they did to him. He never even mentioned it. Fear and guilt made them bring it up. And Joseph gave them a humble reply. He told them that his joy was that many lives had been saved by the adversities he went through because of them. He was not focused on the past.

When David returned from killing Goliath, he did not confront his older brother, "What were you saying earlier? Say it again!" They remembered these things, but rather than making them bitter, they were grateful to God for not putting them to shame. On one hand, they felt relieved. If they had failed the vision, they would have been in hot water! On the other hand, their godly character made them approach the situation from a humble standpoint.

But as for you, you thought evil against me; but God meant it to good, to bring to pass, as it is this day, to save much people alive.

(Genesis 50:20)

LESSON 13: BUILD THE VISION TO BE INDEPENDENT OF YOU

But he [Peter], beckoning to them with the hand to hold their peace, declared to them how the Lord had brought him out of the prison. And he said, Go show these things to James, and to the brethren...

(Acts 12:17)

At this point, Peter had come into the house, and we no longer hear about Rhoda. Peter, the vision, had taken over the show. He came in and asked them not to yell in excitement so as not to attract attention from neighbours. Then he explained how God had miraculously rescued him. Everyone listened in awe. The point here is that you should build your vision to the point where it becomes bigger than you. Build it to the point where it is the vision that dictates proceedings and not you. You want the vision to continue to grow bigger and bigger, therefore, your whims have to shrink further and further. You are no longer chasing personal glory but are willing to step back so that the vision can continue to magnify. That was the secret to John the Baptist's great ministry.

He must increase, but I must decrease.

(John 3:30)

Look at the biggest organisations on earth. They are built by teams. One-man-show organisations never last long after the man is out of the picture. To avoid that, you must build your organisation to survive your resignation, retirement and death. Peter continued to manifest long after we stopped hearing about Rhoda, and this is a lesson for us all.

When you draft in a godly and competent team to help you pursue the vision, you have to let them know your expectations for the project. Bring them to be on the same page with you. They must know that it is not just about you, or the here and now. "The vision must increase and we all must decrease." Once everyone is on the same page, let them express their talents. You will be amazed at what you will achieve when everyone combines their efforts to build the vision. Speaking a common language is a prerequisite for achieving great things. The more everyone on the team is united and on the same page, the bigger the vision grows and the greater your capability. A vision grows to the extent that everyone understands the language of everybody else and stops there. Groups with factions, infighting, and bickering do not achieve much.

And the LORD said, Behold, the people is one, and they have all one language; and this they begin to do: and now, nothing will be restrained from them, which they have imagined to do.

(Genesis 11:5)

Bill Gates stopped being Microsoft's CEO in the year 2000. He stopped being the Chief Software Architect in 2006. And he gave up his position as the Chairman of the Board in 2014. Bill Gates built a team at Microsoft that could continue the vision when he was gone. He gradually withdrew from the organisation so he could focus on other interests. If he had built everything to be about him like many people erroneously do, he would never have been able to retire, and worse, all he built would have collapsed when he left. And no one can be around forever.

Jack Ma's retirement as Executive Chairman of Alibaba was hardly noticed because he had built a strong succession plan over the years. The strong point of this lesson is that you build a strong succession plan to keep the vision alive after you. Succession is the last step of greatness. Many visions have crumbled because they were tied to one powerful entity who left the scene. Let the vision run the show and not you.

LESSON 14: WAIT A MOMENT THEN STRATEGICALLY SHOWCASE THE VISION

*But he, <u>beckoning unto them with the hand to hold their peace</u>,
declared unto them how the Lord had brought him out of the prison.
<u>And he said, Go shew these things unto James, and to the brethren</u>...*

(Acts 12:17)

Now you have successfully achieved the impossible. You braved all odds and invented what only a few believed you could. You landed that scholarship or completed that degree. You completed that production in your bedroom or garage or factory. In addition, you tested the product and it worked just fine as you had imagined it. Congratulations!

The end goal, though, is not to hoard it in your garage or hide it under your bed. You want to circulate it so that it can benefit millions of people. You want the satisfaction of seeing your product in everybody's hands. Maybe you want to commercialise it. At this completion stage, all you have is a sample or prototype or the *minimum viable product* (MVP). You have demonstrated the possibility of the vision on a small scale. You have not circulated it yet. So, now you want to inform everybody about your successful product.

However, at this critical stage, you can lose it all in an instant! Many people have rushed out prematurely to publicise the early success and they watched their labour go up in smoke before their eyes. Do not rush out just yet! Hold your peace and listen for a moment to some final instructions before you go out to publicise the vision! Peter instructed them to hold their peace or keep quiet for a moment.

But he, <u>beckoning unto them with the hand to hold their peace</u>, *declared unto them how the Lord had brought him out of the prison...*

(Acts 12:17)

Why should you hold your peace for a moment? And what should you be doing while holding your peace **before** showcasing the vision? To prevent regrets, you must first establish yourself as the pioneer of the vision. You do this by officially registering the vision in your name. This will prevent others from stealing your idea and taking credit for your labour. You will be surprised how common intellectual theft is in the world. In the United States alone, up to 6,000 intellectual theft lawsuits are filed on average per year. If you have not asserted yourself as the owner of the vision, it can easily be stolen from you and all your reward goes to another.

Moreover, we learnt earlier that others have a similar vision to you. They are dreaming of such a product and are working on a similar idea as yours. If you do not establish yourself as a pioneer, soon enough, someone else will complete their project and establish themselves ahead of you. This is not a case of intellectual theft, they just independently did the same thing as you, sometimes in another country.

No one cares that you came up with the idea first. They only recognise who first patented the product or incorporated the company name. Therefore, to prevent intellectual theft or late arrival, quickly register the idea or product as yours. Patent it. Incorporate the company or reserve the name. Copyright the logo. Do everything it takes to officially establish ownership. These are the acceptable witnesses that it was your idea.

This is also a good time to record all the processes leading to the success of the vision. You want to remember where you have come from and how you got to that point. You want an accurate record of the ingredients of the vision so that you can reproduce the product with the exact same quality. You want an accurate list of contributors so that they can receive the due credit. That was why Peter rehearsed the entire scenario before them to refresh their memory. History is a guide that keeps you from repeating past mistakes and will speed up future efforts. Wait a moment to record your history.

Strategically Showcase the Vision

You have waited and have been guided by the vision on some final instructions and have secured ownership. Now, you can showcase it. Showcasing it creates awareness of your product and clears up assumptions and misconceptions about your vision.

But he, beckoning unto them with the hand to hold their peace, declared unto them how the Lord had brought him out of the prison. And he said, Go shew these things unto James, and to the brethren…

(Acts 12:17)

Someone else could have gone to report to James and the other disciples about some fictitious way that they helped Peter out of prison in a heroic jailbreak. Or James and the brothers may have thought that Peter had been surreptitiously executed. Others may have concluded that Herod had magnanimously released Peter. Yet others may have believed that Peter bribed the guards out of jail. So, Peter wanted everyone to be clear about how he escaped. He instructed the Church, "Go and tell James and the brothers about me. Tell them how your prayers moved the hand of God to save me by an angel. Tell them how you opened the door unto me in the dead of the night. Explain clearly about it and eradicate all doubt and controversy." He instructed them to showcase it, gave them the plan to follow and listed the audience to inform. If you want people to accept it, they must know about it first. No one accepts what they do not know exists.

But he, beckoning unto them with the hand to hold their peace, declared unto them how the Lord had brought him out of the prison. And he said, Go shew these things unto James, and to the brethren…

(Acts 12:17)

Some ways to showcase the vision include:

- a book launch.

- a commissioning ceremony.
- a private exhibition.
- advertising it.
- distributing free or discounted samples.
- marketing it.
- sharing by word of mouth and other means.

We take a cue from Joseph in this regard. When Joseph had perfected his product of interpretation of dreams, he handed out free samples to Pharaoh's chief butler and chief baker. His excellent quality control service had ensured that what he promised was what they got. It was one of those two men that spoke with the king that handed him his big break. He would never have had the chance to hear about the king's dream in the dungeon if he had not freely helped someone that later got his freedom. One day, the need for your product or services will arise outside your circle of influence, and only someone who knows that you do it excellently will be able to recommend you there. Here was the recommendation from the man who got a free sample to showcase the gift:

9 Then spake the chief butler unto Pharaoh, saying…

10 Pharaoh… put me in ward in the captain of the guard's house, both me and the chief baker:

11 And we dreamed a dream in one night, I and he…

12 And there was there with us a young man, an Hebrew, servant to the captain of the guard; and we told him, and he interpreted to us our dreams; to each man according to his dream he did interpret.

13 And it came to pass, as he interpreted to us, so it was; me he restored unto mine office, and him he hanged.

14 Then Pharaoh sent and called Joseph, and they brought him hastily out of the dungeon: and he shaved himself, and changed his raiment, and came in unto Pharaoh.

(Genesis 41:9,12-14)

Again, showcasing the vision must be strategically done. Peter did not say, "Go, show these things to Herod and his soldiers. Go and tell the Jewish leaders." He knew the consequence. Do not showcase it to destroyers (the hostile Jewish and Roman government). Do not showcase it to competitors that will send you out of business (the Jewish religious leaders). Keep away from those you know are wicked. You already know that they are wicked. They will not support you even if you succeed. Why will you keep going back to them to obtain their validation? I hope you see reason in Dan P. Costricone's quote that says, "Reasoning with the unreasonable has no reason."

Enter not into the path of the wicked, and go not in the way of evil men. Avoid it, pass not by it, turn from it, and pass away.

(Proverbs 4:14-15)

Keep away from those who fight your brainchild in the name of protecting religion, culture, and tradition. Cultures and traditions that are not backed by Scripture usually oppose the vision of God.

Making the word of God of none effect through your tradition, which ye have delivered: and many such like things do ye.

(Mark 7:13)

Presenting your vision to bitter critics is like casting your pearls before swine. They will rubbish it and turn around and rip you apart!

Give not that which is holy unto the dogs, neither cast ye your pearls before swine, lest they trample them under their feet, and turn again and rend you.

(Matthew 7:6)

Instead, Peter was deliberate and specific about those he instructed them to tell. "Tell James. Tell the brothers." 'James and the brothers' fall into 6 groups.

Who are 'James and the Brothers'?

(1) They are those who CONTRIBUTED to the vision: James and the other apostles held the fort in Peter's absence. They pastored and encouraged the other distraught and scared Christians. They studied the Word, prayed, and taught the rest. They deserved to be in on it after the miracle. On your way to the top, you must return to appreciate your initial few supporters and cheerleaders because they contributed to your success. Those who gave you the benefit of the doubt or took a chance on you should not be forgotten. Your team, your sponsors, and anyone else who helped you to make it to the finish line must be first on the list.

The husbandman that laboureth must be first partaker of the fruits.

(II Timothy 2:6)

(2) They are those who NEED the vision: James and the other disciples were in sorrow, anxiety, and uncertainty over Peter's arrest and imminent execution. He was one of them and their appointed leader after all. His death would have weakened and demoralised the other apostles and the rest of the Church. They would think, "Who will be executed next after James and Peter? We are powerless against the system." But hearing that Peter had been released from prison would give them great joy and relief. Knowing the miraculous circumstances around it will boost their faith in the power of God. They needed to hear it because they would directly benefit from it. Similarly, there are people who will directly benefit from your vision. In some way, it will make their lives better. They have been yearning so much for a product like yours. It is time to meet their expectation with your manifested vision.

For the earnest expectation of the creature waiteth for the manifestation of the sons of God.

(Romans 8:19)

(3) They are those who will IMPROVE on the vision: There are creative people who will be inspired by your finished product.

They will look at it from different perspectives and suggest improvements. These people will not only benefit from it, but also YOU will benefit from them. These people are included on the list of 'James and the brothers' because you encourage and inspire one another. The Bible lists those who sharpen and improve your vision as your friends.

Iron sharpeneth iron; so a man sharpeneth the countenance of his friend.

(Proverbs 27:17)

(4) They are those who will SPEAK POSITIVELY about the vision: You have learnt to ignore and steer clear of critics, haters, doubters, and naysayers. Surround it with people who speak positively about it. You need people speaking life into it because words are powerful. And you need good publicity. So only those who will build it with words should be drafted in. Those that speak life must eat the fruit of the life they speak.

Death and life are in the power of the tongue: and they that love it shall eat the fruit thereof.

(Proverbs 18:21)

(5) They are those who WANT the vision: These are people who do not desperately need the vision, but who want it for themselves or others nonetheless. Maybe they just like it or they are just curious about it. Maybe they just want to store it up somewhere. Maybe it is one of the numerous options they have. Perhaps someday they will develop the need for it or find an alternative use for it. Since they have indicated positive interest, you should share it with them.

Ask, and it shall be given you; seek, and ye shall find; knock, and it shall be opened unto you: For every one that asketh receiveth; and he that seeketh findeth; and to him that knocketh it shall be opened.

(Matthew 7:7-8)

(6) They are those who will ACCEPT the vision: This category comprises those who neither need it nor want it, but do not hate it either and will accept it if you present it to them. They are neutral but open to your idea. At some point, they too may need it. If it is very good, they may like it. So, if you present it to neutrals and they accept it, let them have it. If they reject it, leave them alone. It doesn't matter if they need it: if they do not accept it, they should be left out.

And when ye come into an house, salute it. And whosoever shall not receive you, nor hear your words, when ye depart out of that house or city, shake off the dust of your feet.

(Matthew 10:12,14)

LESSON 15: THE VISION GOES OUT AGAIN

...And he departed, and went into another place.

(Acts 12:17)

Just as Peter went out to another place after manifesting to the brethren in Mary's house, the vision does not remain with you permanently. After you deliver the initial vision, it goes out to others. You caught and delivered the first form or version, the 'Vision 1.0'. You have showcased it publicly. Now, everyone sees the possibility. They see how it works and functions. Then they start imagining tweaks, improvements, insights, and alternative uses for it. They start to catch their own vision from your delivered vision. Therefore, the vision goes out again to seek out other visioners seeing a new manifestation to continue from where you stopped. This way, the 'Vision 2.0', 'Vision 3.0', etc., are developed.

Look at any invention in the world today—computers, cars, motorbikes, bicycles, books, houses, telephones, televisions, refrigerators, internet, camera, guns, etc. You will discover that the initial invention was much different and almost unrecognisable compared to what you see today. There is a continuum of development going on from the first inventor through others over the years who kept updating and improving the invention until we have today's products.

Take computers for example. Today, they are everywhere, from digital wristwatches to computerised fuel pumps. The average weight of a desktop computer is about 10 kg (laptops weigh only about 2 kg on average, and smartphones weigh between 0.14 kg and 0.2 kg). But believe it or not, the first computer designed by Charles Babbage in 1822 measured 8 feet tall and weighed 13,600 kg, which is equivalent to 1,360 desktops, or 6,800 laptops, or 75,556 smartphones, or a heavy-duty truck with 24 to 36 tyres! Yet, this computer was very limited in function. It was not even called a computer. It was known as the Difference Engine because it could only perform arithmetic and polynomial functions. It multiplied or divided indirectly by performing repeated additions or subtractions and that takes time. It had no memory capacity or display screen like today's devices.

His second computer was a smaller model and minor upgrade to the first. It weighed about a third of the first model, and took a team of engineers six years to build only one of it! It was known as the Analytical Engine because it could multiply and divide directly in addition to arithmetic and polynomial functions.

The third computer developed by Babbage was called the Difference Engine No. 2. It was 15 feet tall—about 2.5 times the average height of a man—and 20 feet long! That would only fit in a hall (Babbage designed computers of ten times this size!). As with the others, it could only be powered by steam engine because of the energy it consumed. It took this computer 3 minutes to multiply two 20-digit numbers. Despite its humongous size, its memory capacity was only 675 **bytes**. For context, 1024 bytes make 1 kilobyte (KB), 1024 KB make 1 megabyte (MB), and 1024 MB make 1 gigabyte. Results were printed out but there was no display screen.

Babbage spent a lot of effort trying to convince people to accept his idea. After a while, his source of funding from the British Government was cut off because they did not believe in his ideas. He became financially stranded. He never actually completed a prototype of any of his computers in his lifetime because of this lack of funding and support. But he did his best to showcase his vision publicly and get credited as the Father of the Computer. Only a few people associated with him. Like every pioneer like Rhoda, he faced stiff opposition and huge frustration. Gradually, more and more individuals and groups started realising the potentials of his machines.

My point is that, over time, many people started conceiving new ideas to add to the computer. So, the vision went out to them all one by one, just like Peter left the original house where he stopped.

"We can reduce its steam energy consumption."

"We can power it with electricity."

"We can use it to compute results of our national census instead of doing it manually which is slow, tedious, and error-prone."

"We can find computer applications in military vessels like aircraft and submarines."

"We can introduce a display screen so that we can see the results on a screen."

"We can make it a bit smaller."

"We can make the display screen show us the data we enter and not only the output."

"We can develop the internet that gives the computer information through satellites."

"We can increase the memory capacity and make it store information for longer."

"We can produce it with cheaper materials."

"We can create external memory devices to easily transfer data between computers."

"We can have a computer small enough to fit on a desk."

"We can commercialise computers and make them affordable to the general public."

"We can computerise everyday devices like watches, telephones, cameras, and even doors."

"We can have a computer that fits on the laps."

"We can have tiny, handheld computers."

"We can make robots that can perform human functions."

And so on.

The vision went out to all of them one by one for improvement, and they manifested it.

...And he departed, and went into another place.

(Acts 12:17)

So, for over 200 years, with the combined innovation of several generations of mathematicians, engineers, the military, businessmen, applied scientists, and innovators from all walks of life, computers have progressively reduced in size and increased in speed and utility. Today, a micro memory card weighing the same as a feather can have a 1-terabyte (1024 GB) memory capacity, approximately 1.63 **billion** times the capacity of Babbage's 20-foot monstrosity.

A major indicator of growth is how different the device is today compared to the original invention. And that is evident in the computer. You can also see it in other inventions like automobiles and aircraft, to mention only two. Innovation continued with others.

Almost everything has been computerised today. Robots paint football fields and attend to you in a restaurant. Supermarkets are trimming down staff size due to increased computerisation of the shopping process. You make phone calls and text with your wristwatch. Charles Babbage's rejected invention is an inseparable part of today's world. But also, more people added their own ideas to his vision.

Of course, you should also strive to improve on your own invention, and in that case, it will return to you again at some point. This is common in business. But everyone sees from a different perspective and others will imagine things that you did not. Hence, at the very least, actively source for feedback from your users and encourage them to get back to you. You will be surprised at the resourceful improvements they will suggest.

Notice that it becomes easier to improve when there is something already on ground. It is easier to enhance than to build from scratch. We must celebrate pioneers because they fight harder battles to land a vision than others that come after. Others just have to continue from where they stopped. This time, the vision is no longer in chains surrounded by soldiers, although it is still in peril. It does not need another spectacular jailbreak. It is easier to hide in the city than to break out of jail with chains on your hands in a cell full of soldiers. Inventors, founders, and pioneers must be honoured. They are the fathers and mothers of difficult processes. They scaled through difficult situations. Many die in the process and never live to reap the fruit of their labour. Their contributions must be documented for the next generation to read. Moses received the commandment that we should honour fathers and mothers, or pioneers of an idea (Exodus 20:12). Jesus repeated it (Matthew 15:4; Mark 7:10). Paul repeated it (Ephesians 6:2). Then it must be very important and we must not forget it.

Honour thy father and mother; which is the first commandment with promise;

(Ephesians 6:2)

The point in this lesson is that there is always room for improvement on your vision and the visions of others. The vision goes out again to whoever imagines something new. So, never stop imagining and never stop improving on the status quo.

FOUR OUTCOMES OF A VISION
WHEN IT IS PLANTED

Hearken; Behold, there went out a sower to sow:

(Mark 4:3)

The Bible equates catching a vision to conception or getting pregnant. Therefore, the vision is like a seed that lands upon a man's heart. It is sown into people's hearts by the Spirit of God or by normal life processes such as the presence of visible deficiencies. The outcome of the vision does not depend on the seed, because the seed is good and fertile. The outcome depends on the kind of soil (heart) upon which it lands.

In the parable of the sower, Jesus told us four possible outcomes that can happen to a vision when it knocks on the door of people's hearts. We will study this parable in this chapter and understand each category from the standpoint of manifesting a vision.

Hearken; Behold, there went out a sower to sow:

(Mark 4:3)

(1) It is rejected by the receiver:

And it came to pass, as he sowed, some fell by the way side, and the fowls of the air came and devoured it up.

(Mark 4:4)

The first group of people comprises those who do not understand the vision and never pay attention to it or allow it to settle in their hearts. They reject it immediately or soon after. It also includes those who DO understand the vision but intentionally reject it. These are people who do not think that the vision is worth pursuing or worth their time. They have other important things to pursue. Therefore, the vision is stolen from their hearts by Satan, hate, disillusionment, ignorance, or whatever.

When any one heareth the word of the kingdom [the vision], *and understandeth it not, then cometh the wicked one, and catcheth away that which was sown in his heart. This is he which received seed by the way side.*

(Matthew 13:19)

This also applies to a bad vision that is planted by the enemy, the flesh, or an imposition of men. Instead of nursing it and allowing it grow to maturity, you weed it out quickly before it grows roots.

But while men slept, his enemy came and sowed tares among the wheat, and went his way.

(Matthew 13:25)

Then the "birds of the air" may be idea thieves and plagiarisers who run ahead of the original visioner and leave the initial recipient with nothing.

(2) It fails because it is attempted by men without capacity:

And some fell on stony ground, where it had not much earth; and immediately it sprang up, because it had no depth of earth: But when the sun was up, it was scorched; and because it had no root, it withered away.

(Mark 4:5-6)

The second group is made up of those who receive the vision but lack the capacity to bring it to reality. First, the Bible likens them to stony ground. The stony ground is encumbered by all kinds of stones of impatience, immaturity, fear, unbelief, showmanship, pride, gluttony, and personal weaknesses that combat the vision from within. The presence of unwanted factors in their life and personality takes up space for fertile soil and the stones burn out the vision.

Then the Bible says that they lack depth. They do not have what it takes to get it right. They lack the inner girth and skills to correctly pursue the vision. And rather than taking the time to learn what they should and build depth, they rush headlong into it. As a result, they run ahead of their capacity and resources and soon get stuck. Before long, the heat of running the vision starts to burn them. When the storms of life come like the heat of the sun, the vision is scorched to death because they lack depth, and they return to square one.

But he that received the seed into stony places, the same is he that heareth the word, and anon with joy receiveth it; Yet hath he not root in himself, but dureth for a while: for when tribulation or persecution ariseth because of the word, by and by he is offended.

(Matthew 13:20-21)

Men and women who want to be seen and heard very quickly fall into this category. They lack the patience to settle down and build themselves, and they soon lose it all. Before you go out there, be sure to be deeply rooted and adequately prepared for the assignment, because the heat will come. It always does! Abraham Lincoln said, "If I am given twenty-four hours to cut down a tree, I will spend twenty hours sharpening my axe." This shows how important preparation and capacity development are in chasing your life's goals. Haste makes waste.

(3) It fails because it is crowded out:

And some fell among thorns, and the thorns grew up, and choked it, and it yielded no fruit.

(Mark 4:7)

The third outcome is that the vision is eagerly received, the recipient has sufficient capacity to handle it and they start running with the vision. But these people lack focus. They do not give adequate attention to the vision. It is just one of many options that they are exploring. Among a million other things that have their attention, the vision suffocates to death. Look back at all the great ideas you have had in the past. Did you have time to nurse them to reality? You may say, "I just had no time to continue doing it." The vision had been choked to death by other priorities. For some people, it is threats and fear that choke out the vision. Maybe it is a health challenge or some other factors beyond their control. Many people I have spoken to fall in this category. They say they are very busy and cannot pursue their ideas.

He also that received seed among the thorns is he that heareth the word; and the care of this world, and the deceitfulness of riches, choke the word, and he becometh unfruitful.

(Matthew 13:22)

(4) It succeeds:

And other fell on good ground, and did yield fruit that sprang up and increased; and brought forth, some thirty, and some sixty, and some an hundred.

(Mark 4:8)

The final outcome of a vision is that it succeeds. The heart is right. The recipient is prepared. They make out the time, and they give the vision full focus. They wait patiently to grow the vision, and slowly, it starts to mature before their eyes. This may take some time, depending on many factors like the kind and size of the vision.

But he that received seed into the good ground is he that heareth the word, and understandeth it; which also beareth fruit, and bringeth forth, some an hundredfold, some sixty, some thirty.

(Matthew 13:23)

We see also that the yield is not the same for everyone. The extent of your yield depends on the ground, that is, the recipient. It depends on you. How do you receive and run with the vision? How much preparedness and focus went into it? Even among those who bring it to the point of yield, we see three levels of yield. These are thirtyfold, sixtyfold, and a hundredfold. We may call that

30%, 60%, and 100% yield. These three figures can be classified into three categories:

a. Below average yield: They enjoy some yield but it is low and way below the maximum capacity.

b. Average to above average yield: They get more than the bare minimum but do not get the full capacity of yield.

c. Excellent yield: They go all the way and get the maximum yield from the vision.

FIVE REASONS WHY YOU MUST PURSUE THE VISION

Where there is no vision, the people perish: but
he that keepeth the law, happy is he.

(Proverbs 29:18)

You must catch the vision. And that in itself is insufficient. You must run with it and obtain it. Here are five reasons why you must deliver your God-given vision to this world:

(1) You must pursue the vision because the world is perishing: You must catch a vision and pursue it! *Where there is no vision, the people perish.* The people weep! The people suffer! The people mourn! The people are dying! There are so many problems in the world today. People are sad, depressed, blind, frustrated, heartbroken, demoralised, displaced, suicidal, poor, broken, robbed, deceived, maimed, and destroyed. There are natural and artificial disasters all over the globe. The whole creation is groaning!

For we know that the whole creation groaneth and travaileth in pain together until now.

(Romans 8:22)

What do we need? We need saviours. We yearn for the manifestation of men with visions. Being a Christian is not enough. You must be a manifesting Christian. The world needs people to lift them out of darkness, pain, and distress. We need more problem-solvers. Talk is cheap. We need more people that will bring imaginations to reality.

For the earnest expectation of the creature waiteth for the manifestation of the sons of God.

(Romans 8:19)

You cannot do everything. The government cannot do everything. No one has all the solutions. But if everyone focused on their vision rather than idling around or sticking their nose inside other people's business, more solutions and relief will come to the world day by day. You must pursue your vision to stop the world from suffering and perishing. When you manifest your vision and men get relief from their tears and suffering, they will glorify God because of you.

Let your light so shine before men, that they may see your good works, and glorify your Father which is in heaven.

(Matthew 5:16)

(2) You must pursue the vision because the vision benefits you personally: While the vision makes you an easy target, it comes with tremendous personal benefits. Having a vision you are pursuing transforms you. It gives your life a focus which keeps you busy from many sins and vices in society. You are absorbed into a project that takes most or all of your time. Because of that, you think differently. You have no time for frivolities. You are dedicated to seeing it through and seeing it work. You are resolute not to fail at it. In the process of chasing the vision, you are set apart and you are saved from many problems.

Having a great imagination which you want to achieve gives you hope. I can almost tell a man with a vision from one without a vision from the words they say and the way they lead their lives. A man with a vision has many challenges but is less prone to hopelessness because his life has a purpose. Many hopeless and despondent people are people without a vision. They have nothing to look forward to. The vision gives you another reason to live.

The vision will more often than not bring you into the limelight. It will open doors of opportunity to you that will never be available to the lazy person who spends all his time plugged into entertainment gadgets. Your loved ones will benefit from it too. It is time to start reaping the benefits of pursuing the vision. It may make you rich. It may give you a good name. It may immortalise you. It may open good doors for your children. Oh, my brother, oh my sister, you must pursue your vision!

Where there is no vision, the people perish: but he that keepeth the law [he that follows the vision], happy [fortunate, blessed, favoured] is he.

(Proverbs 29:18)

(3) You must pursue the vision because you will give account of your life: You will give account of your life when you stand before God. He will ask you about all the ideas and visions that He gave you throughout your lifetime. He will question you on what you did about the various solutions He put in your heart to accomplish to relieve the pain and sorrow on earth. What will you tell your Maker when the time comes?

So then every one of us shall give account of himself to God.

(Romans 14:12)

Will it not be shameful that among all the numerous beautiful imaginations you had all through your life, you never did anything about any of them? You were only concerned about making money and developing your own life alone. What a selfish way to live! Brethren, God wants to help the world through us, and He will ask us when our time is up!

(4) You must pursue the vision to prevent regrets: Time is running out on you. You have an expiration date. You cannot do anything extra when you are dead. Now is the only time that you have to do anything meaningful. You will wake up one day and realise that your time here is about to end, and you will look back on your life. I have heard that above all other regrets, what haunts people the most at the point of their death are the things that they ought to have accomplished but never did. They regret the wasted opportunities to do more and be more.

Now Joshua was old and stricken in years: and the LORD said unto him, Thou art old and stricken in years, and there remaineth yet very much land to be possessed.

(Joshua 13:1)

God did not say, "Joshua, see how much land you have already obtained! What a good job you've done!" No. God compared what Joshua had done with what remained to be done, and God concluded that Joshua had not achieved much in His plan.

I believe that this is how God will relate to each one of us when our time to depart this world draws near. If you are privileged to be able to do something now, now is your chance. It would be very sad for you to lie on your deathbed weeping that you never reached your maximum potential for excuses that do not hold water. The mistakes you made while trying to achieve your vision will pale in comparison to the regret of never amounting to what you should have. You may achieve your vision, and you may not. But the fear of failure must never stop you from pursuing God's vision for your life.

Highly focused men like Jesus and Paul knew that time was running out. They wanted to avoid the regret of knowing that they could have done more. And so, they chased the vision passionately and vigorously. When their time was up, they knew that they had done everything that God wanted them to do. With a sense of fulfilment, Jesus said, "It is finished" (John 19:30), and Paul said, "I have finished my course." (II Timothy 4:7). Will you finish your course?

(5) You must pursue the vision because it is achievable: God has not retired from the business of doing the impossible. And He will never ask you to do what He has not empowered you to do. You have an illustrious bunch of divinely assisted visionaries to look up to. The vision that you carry may be bigger than you, but it is not bigger than God. Do not allow the fear of failure to scare you from doing what God has commissioned you to do. The same God who helped the fathers of old is alive. Partner with Him and you will surmount the insurmountable in your life. Secular men apply life's principles to achieve their vision even though they do not believe in God. Why should you then be afraid when you have God by your side? Believe that the vision is possible through Christ in you. Go and get it, I believe in you!

I can do all things through Christ which strenghteneth me.

(Philippians 4:13)

Jesus said unto him, If thou canst believe, all things are possible to him that believeth. And Jesus looking upon them saith, With men it is impossible, but not with God: for with God all things are possible.

(Mark 9:23, 10:27)

INVITATION

I cordially invite you to join my official online community. There, I discuss the contents of this and other books I have written. You also enjoy a lot of Christian content that I have not published, and you have the opportunity to share your thoughts via comments or direct messages. An added advantage is that you will be informed when I publish a new book.

Instagram: @word.oesokefun
YouTube: oesokefun

Finally, all my books are available on Amazon worldwide. I invite you to get them there. Please, don't forget to leave honest and helpful reviews of the product. If you have been blessed by my content, please inform others about them and get them as gifts for your friends and family so that they too will be blessed. They will be grateful you did!

NOTES

NOTES

ABOUT THE AUTHOR

O. Emmanuel Sokefun

 is a teacher of God's Word, a minister in the Redeemed Christian Church of God, and a biomedical sciences researcher. He has a B.Sc. in microbiology from Redeemer's University and an M.Sc. in microbiology from Covenant University.

Made in the USA
Columbia, SC
11 June 2024

36307897R10054